AF480089

About the Author

Jude Simon is an artist who creates in several art styles including work working, sculpting, and painting. Now Jude has taken his passion for creativity to a love letter to his children. In his debut book "What Will You Be?", he wants to use his art to encourage everyone to explore their passions and curiosities but most importantly, to be themselves.

To my unborn child, I love you more than you will ever know!

WHAT WILL YOU BE?

Written and Illustrated
by
Jude Simon

When you arrive in this world, what will you be?

Will you be big or small, short or tall?

Will you grow like a weed
or take your time like a seed?

Will you frolic and play?
Will you laugh all day?

Will your smile be contagious?
Will your words be courageous?

Will you love food and learn to cook?

Will you love to read and write a book?

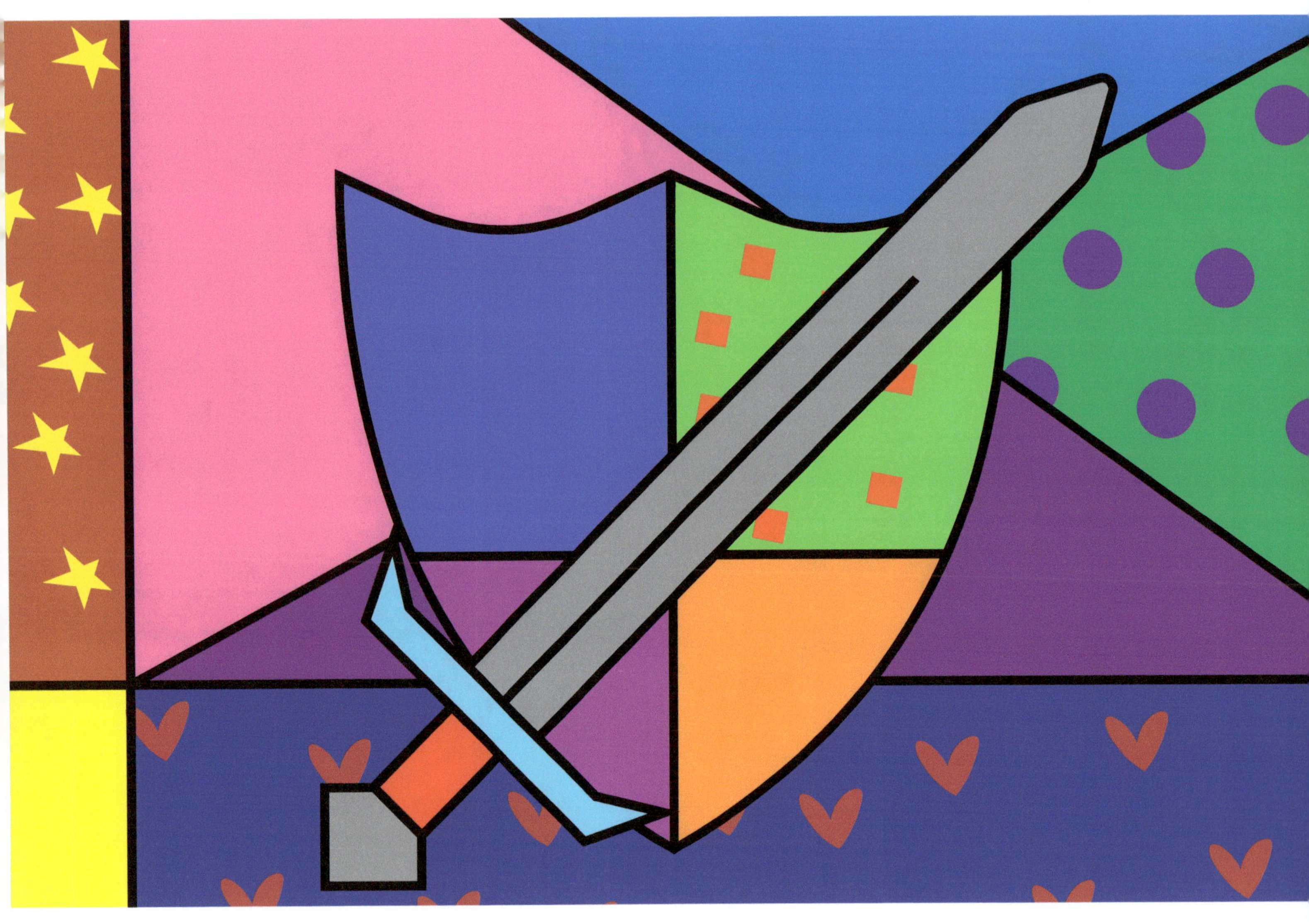

Will you be brave and show no fear?

Will you pump up a crowd and make people cheer?

Will you pump up a crowd and make people cheer?

Will you teach the world about something new?

Will we see your name in lights?
Will you travel to new heights?

Will you make it out to space?
Will you earn a new first place?

Will you paint or draw?
Will you study the law?

Will you act and perform?
Will you teach and inform?

Will you use your voice to sing a song?
Will you make people feel like they belong?

Will you spin and leap through the air?
Will you dance like no one is there?

My child, whatever you will be,
know this to be true.

The best thing in the world you can be
the one and only...

YOU